RELIGIONS

Robert Fisher

Macdonald Educational

How to use this book

First, look at the contents page opposite. Read the chapter list to see if it includes the subject you want. The list tells you what each page is about. You can then find the page with the information you need.

If you want to know about one particular thing, look it up in the index on page 31. For example, if you want to know about Buddhism, the index tells you that there is something about it on page 11. The index also lists the pictures in the book.

When you read this book, you will find some unusual words. The glossary on page 30 explains what they mean.

Series Editor
Margaret Conroy

Book Editor
Polly Dunnett

Series Design
Robert Mathias/Anne Isseyegh

Book Design
Danuta Trebus

Production
Marguerite Fenn

Picture Research
Caroline Mitchell

Factual Adviser
Owen Cole

Reading Consultant
Amy Gibbs

Teacher Panel
Diana Foster, John Allen,
Ann Merriman

Illustrations
Graham Allen/Linden Artists, 6-7
Jeremy Gower/ B. L. Kearley, 10-11, 15
Kate Rogers 12-13, 16-17, 29

Photographs
Andes Press Agency: 21
Barnaby's Picture Library: 26T
Bridgeman Art Library: 13
Hutchison Library: 14, 15, 27T, 29
Christine Osborne: 18, 20
Bury Peerless: Cover
Pictorial Press: 11
David Richardson: 23
Liba Taylor: 19, 24
ZEFA: 6, 8, 9, 17, 22–23, 25, 26B, 27B

CONTENTS

BELIEFS

What is religion?

There are many things in life that are mysterious and difficult for us to understand. How did the world begin? What happens when we die? Why should we try to be good? These are some of the questions that people have always asked. Perhaps you too have thought about them and wondered what the answers are.

Religions help people to answer some of these difficult and important questions. They teach people what to believe and how to lead good lives. Many people find answers to their questions in religion. Their religion is a way of living. Other people do not believe in any religion, but they still ask questions and try to find their own answers.

Long ago, people worshipped the Sun. Stonehenge was built about 4000 years ago, and may have been used as a place to worship the Sun.

Long ago people thought up stories about invisible gods and spirits that made things happen in the world. These stories became part of their religion. They described how the world was made and what happens when people die. They also taught people how to behave.

There are many different religions in the world. They give different answers to the important questions people ask, but they all try to do the same thing. They all try to explain the mysteries of life and show people how they should live.

Some people once thought a spirit, or goddess, lived in the growing corn. After the harvest, they made the last of the corn into a 'corn dolly', to keep the spirit alive in winter.

How religions begin

If you ask someone a question they cannot answer they may say, 'God knows'. They mean that the question is so hard, no one could know the answer except God. Most religions believe in God or gods who made the world and who know everything. Some religions have only one God. Others have many gods and goddesses. Sometimes God is spoken of as 'He' or 'Father'. But in different religions God has different names. Some religions, including most kinds of Buddhism, have no god at all.

This huge statue of the Buddha was built for a Buddhist temple in Japan. The Buddha, founder of Buddhism, lived in India 2500 years ago.

Many religions were started by one person, called a founder. The founder of Christianity was Jesus of Nazareth. He lived about 2000 years ago and Christians believe he was both 'Son of God' and 'Son of Man', that is, he was both God and a human being.

Judaism was founded by prophets, or messengers of God, such as the prophet Abraham. They said the Jews were the chosen people of God. The founder of the Sikh religion was Guru Nanak. He lived in the Punjab region of India about 500 years ago. Some religions, like Hinduism, have no particular founder.

Religions that began in one country have usually spread to others. When people travel to live in a new country they often take their religion with them. People who believe in a religion are called its followers. The biggest religions now have millions of followers all over the world.

The founder of Islam was the prophet Muhammad. He was born in Makkah, or Mecca, which is the holy city of the Muslim religion. Here Muslims gather round the Ka'aba, the shrine at the centre of the mosque in Makkah.

Different traditions

Each religion has its own beliefs, stories, customs, or ways of doing things, and rules about how to live, which have all been handed down from the past. These are called traditions. Many traditions are thousands of years old.

Different religions started in different parts of the world. Judaism, Christianity and Islam all started in the Middle East, and these three religions share some of their traditions.

The six best-known religions in the world today are Christianity, Islam, Hinduism, Buddhism, Sikhism and Judaism.

**Six
World
Religions**

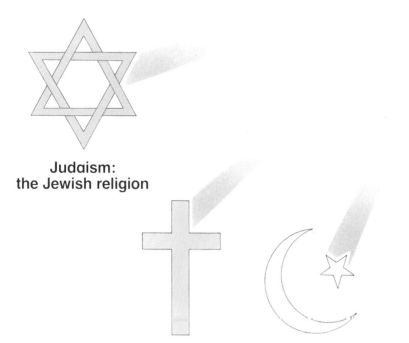

Judaism:
the Jewish religion

Christianity:
the Christian religion

Islam:
the Muslim religion

Sikhism:
the Sikh religion

These schoolchildren probably belong to many different religions.

For example, the Christian holy book, the Bible, contains the history and beliefs of the ancient Jews as well as the story of Jesus.

Another group of religions started in India. These include Hinduism, Buddhism and Sikhism. And in the Far Eastern countries of China and Japan there are some very ancient religions, such as the Shinto religion. Many other religions grew up among the tribal peoples of Africa, Australia and America.

Some religions have died out, like those of the ancient Egyptians, Greeks and Romans. Others, such as the Ba'hai or the Mormon religions, are quite new. They have grown up in the last 150 years.

In some countries, most of the people follow the same religion. For example, in Arab countries, most people are Muslims. In other countries there are many different religions.

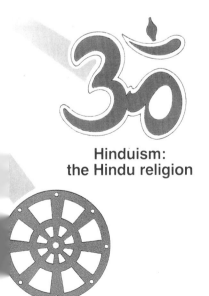

Hinduism: the Hindu religion

Buddhism: Buddhist religion

11

Stories and beliefs

All religions have their own special stories, which help to explain what the religion is about, and show people what to believe and how to behave. Many religions have stories about how the world was created, or made. The Aboriginal people of Australia have a name for the time when the world was created. They call it the Dreamtime, and their Dreamtime stories help to explain the world and teach them how to live.

Many religious stories show how goodness and truth can overcome evil. The Hindu story about the god Rama and his wife Sita is one example. The hero Rama rescued Sita by killing the demon king Ravana. Rama was able to kill the demon because he had faith, or strong beliefs. Stories like these encourage people to have faith in their religion.

Hindus believe that God has many forms. There are special stories and beliefs about each one. The god Shiva is shown here dancing on the body of a demon. The goddess Parvati is Shiva's wife. The god Vishnu is the preserver of life, and he also appears in other forms, such as the heroes Rama and Krishna.

Parvati

Vishnu

Christians learn stories about the life of Jesus. This painting shows the story of the birth of Jesus, or his 'nativity'. Wise men came to offer gifts to the baby Jesus, who was born in a stable.

A religion may have stories about its founder. Buddhists learn the story of the Buddha's life. He gave up being a rich prince to try and find out the truth about life. He taught people to be kind and thoughtful, not selfish and greedy.

Religious stories may also describe a perfect place, sometimes called heaven, where people go when they die. For Eskimos, this is a place where the Sun always shines. American Indians call it the 'happy hunting ground'.

Many religions have people whose job is to lead the prayers and worship. These people also help followers to understand the stories of their religion, and what they teach. Christians have a priest or minister, Jews have a rabbi, and Muslims have an imam.

Shiva

WORSHIP

Sacred places

People worship what they think is important and of real worth. Worshipping means showing that you value someone or something very highly indeed. In most religions people worship God. They do this by reading holy books, by praying, by having special celebrations, by following certain customs or by visiting holy places. Worship is a very important part of all religions.

Every religion has special places, just for worship. They are often beautiful buildings where people can go and feel close to God. Muslims have a mosque, Jews have a synagogue, Hindus have a temple, Sikhs have a gurdwara or temple and Christians have a church or chapel.

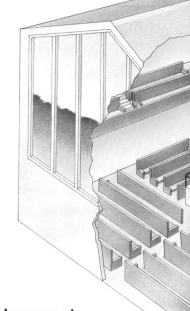

Jews meet for worship in a building called a synagogue. Here you can see the inside of a synagogue. The Ark curtain covers a cupboard which contains the Jewish holy book, the Torah.

For Hindus, the River Ganges in India is sacred. Here pilgrims bathe in the Ganges at Benares.

14

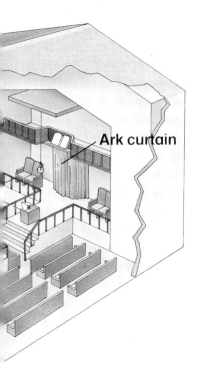

Ark curtain

All these places are special to the people who go to worship there. They are called 'sacred' or 'holy' places because they are specially important in the religion. When they enter a sacred building, people show their care and respect in different ways. For example, in some religions people take off their shoes, or cover their heads, or talk in a whisper.

Some places are sacred because of things that happened there. People who make special journeys there are called pilgrims. Every year millions of Muslim pilgrims travel to their holy city of Makkah, or Mecca, in Saudi Arabia. For Christians the country of Israel is special because Jesus lived there, and so they call it the 'Holy Land.' The city of Jerusalem in Israel is a holy city for three religions: for Jews, Muslims and Christians.

The Golden Temple at Amritsar in India is a sacred place for Sikhs. Many thousands of pilgrims visit it every year.

The lotus flower is a symbol of Buddhism. It reminds Buddhists of the life and teachings of the Buddha.

Symbols

When people use your name they mean YOU. Your name stands for something — it is a sign or symbol for you. There are many other kinds of symbol that stand for all kinds of different things. A school badge is a symbol for a school. Numbers are symbols that we use every day.

Colours can be used as symbols, too. Red is the symbol for danger in traffic signals. Objects and actions can also be signs or symbols. A wedding ring is a symbol of a married couple's promise to love each other and stay together. Kissing is a sign of love.

This girl wears a cross on her necklace. The cross is a symbol for Christians because it reminds them how Jesus died.

Every religion has its own symbols. You can see some of them on pages 10 and 11. Religious symbols stand for something important in a religion. For example, Hindus and Buddhists use the wheel as a symbol. They believe that we die and are born again as a different person or animal. They believe life goes on like this in a kind of circle, which is called the Wheel of Life. For Jews, the star of David is an important symbol. It has many meanings. One is that the points of the star stand for human beings reaching up to God, and for God reaching down to human beings. The most holy symbol for Muslims is the beautifully-written name of God, whom they call Allah.

Other symbols like light, water, food and flowers are used in many different religions. Symbols remind people of what is important in life and religion. They are something for people to share and think about.

The menorah is a symbol for Jewish people. It is a candle-holder, usually with seven branches. The menorah in this picture has eight branches because it is a special one for the festival of Hanukah.

Books and writings

Do you have a special book, one that is more important to you than any other? Most religions have books and writings which are special and sacred. They are sometimes called scriptures. They tell people what to believe and how to live their lives. Often they contain stories and teachings, which people believe are God's special message to them.

The holy book of the Sikhs is called the Guru Granth Sahib. It is always kept in a place of honour in a Sikh temple. It may be read aloud by any Sikh man or woman. The Sikh in this picture is waving a fan over the holy book as a sign of respect.

Muslim girls learning to read from the Qu'ran, which is written in Arabic.

People treat their sacred books with great care. The Qu'ran is the holy book of the Muslims. They believe it contains the actual words of Allah, which the angel Gabriel told to Muhammad. The Qu'ran is usually wrapped in a silk cloth to protect it, and should only be touched with clean hands. A family will keep their copy of the Qu'ran on a high shelf so that no other book can be placed above it.

Sacred writings can include stories, history, wise sayings, rules about what to do, letters, songs, poems and prayers. People can read them, sing them, chant them or recite them from memory. Sacred books can be used in many ways. When Christians take an oath in a court of law, promising to tell the truth, they hold their sacred book, the Bible. This shows that they really mean their promise. When people worship together, they often read some part of their holy book. They may also keep a copy of their holy book at home to read and learn from.

Prayers and sayings

Do you ever pray or say prayers? Many people do. Prayer is a special kind of thinking or saying. It is a way of talking and listening to God. Prayers are an important part of worship in most religions.

There are many different reasons for praying. People pray to show their love of God. They pray because they want to thank God for the goods things of life. They pray to ask for help when things go wrong, or when they want to know what to do next. Sometimes people want to say sorry for what they have done wrong.

There are many different ways of praying. People can say prayers out loud, or sing them, or say them silently to themselves. They can repeat prayers that they have already learnt, or they can make up their own words.

Muslims should pray five times a day, facing towards their holy city of Makkah. This woman kneels on her prayer mat, holding beads to help her concentrate on her prayers.

People may pray together or they may pray alone. They may pray at important times of the day; for example, at dawn, at meal-times, or before bedtime. They may kneel, stand or sit to pray. In many religions, people pray with their eyes closed. All these different ways of praying help people to concentrate on God and on their prayers.

Instead of praying, some people meditate. Meditating means concentrating very hard on one idea and clearing your mind of all other thoughts. There are different kinds of meditating in different religions.

Sometimes people from different religions gather together to pray for something special. These Buddhists are in a Christian church, praying for peace in the world.

Rituals and customs

How did you start your day today? Many religious people begin each day with an act of worship. For example, they might say a prayer of thanks to God. Doing something special at certain times of the day helps them to express their religious feelings and to remember what is important in their religion. Any special set of actions that mean something religious are called rituals.

Each religion has its own rituals. They may include visiting holy places, praying, singing sacred songs, giving presents or offerings to God, or reading holy books. Candles are often used to show that the ritual is holy. Water is also used in many rituals. It is a symbol for cleanliness and goodness. Muslims and Hindus always wash before praying.

People may make special movements in their rituals, such as kneeling or bowing down to show their respect for God. Dancing, or acting plays, may also be rituals. American Indians do a ritual dance called the Sun Dance and Hindus perform plays that tell stories about their gods.

All these rituals are special things that people do at special times. There are other rituals, and also customs, that are part of the way people live their everyday lives.

Christians in Africa take part in an open-air Mass. At Mass, or Holy Communion, Christians share bread, and sometimes wine, in memory of Jesus' last meal with his close followers, or disciples.

Many religious customs are about food. Sikhs share a meal after meeting in the temple or gurdwara. Some people may not be allowed to eat certain foods. For example, Muslims and Jews must not eat pork.

Many religions also have customs about clothing. For example, Sikhs should wear a bracelet on their right wrist, and should not cut their hair. Sikh men should also wear a turban. Customs and rituals help people to make their religion a way of life.

A Hindu family worship at a shrine in their home. A family shrine has pictures of Hindu gods, and offerings of flowers or food. The family say prayers together every morning.

CELEBRATIONS

Holy days

Do you enjoy holidays? Long ago, the only holidays were 'holy days'. They were days in each year kept specially for worship or celebrations. People did no work on those days. Most religions still have holy days, although nowadays people have other holidays as well.

Some religions have a holy day each week. For Jews, it is the seventh day of each week. They call it the Sabbath, and it lasts from sunset on Friday to sunset on Saturday. Sunday is the holy day for Christians and they usually have a special 'service' when they meet together for worship in a church or chapel. Friday is the holy day for Muslims. On Friday, all Muslims try to go to midday prayers at the mosque.

On Good Friday, Christians think about the death of Jesus. These Christians in Mexico are acting the story of the last day of Jesus' life.

A Jewish family meal on Friday evening, at the start of the Sabbath.

Hindus, Sikhs and Buddhists do not have any special day of the week as a holy day. And some religious people worship every day, thinking of all days as holy.

Many religions celebrate special holy days at certain times every year. Jews have Passover, which is the time when they remember how they escaped from slavery in Egypt, thousands of years ago. Muslims have a holy month called Ramadan, when they eat no food from dawn to dusk. They spend time reading the Qu'ran and thinking about their religion. Two very special days for Christians are Good Friday, when Jesus died, and Easter Sunday, when he rose from the dead.

Family life

Does your family ever come together to celebrate something special? Perhaps it is a birthday or someone is getting married. Family celebrations are important in all religions. Religion is a way of life, so religious people celebrate special family times in a religious way.

Families like to celebrate the birth of a new baby. Many parents present their baby before God in a church or temple. There may be a special ceremony, when the baby is given a name. Some religions have another ceremony, when the child is older, and ready to become a full member of the religion.

These Christian parents have brought their baby to church for baptism. Being baptized marks the beginning of a person's life as a Christian.

A Jewish Bar Mitzvah ceremony. The boy is becoming a full member of the Jewish religion.

Another important day in the lives of many people is their wedding day. A lot of people get married in a place of worship, where they can ask God to help make their lives together good and happy.

Families usually come together when one of the family dies. In most religions, death is not the end, but the beginning of a new and different kind of life. Each religion has its own special ceremony for this time, called a funeral. Muslims wrap the body of the dead person in sheets and carry it to the mosque for prayers before they bury it. Hindus cremate, or burn, the body, with special prayers and songs, or hymns.

A Sikh wedding ceremony takes place in a gurdwara, or temple, in front of the sacred book, the Guru Granth Sahib.

There are many other times when families get together for a religious celebration, such as holy days and festivals. Family life is important in all religions. Showing love and care for your family is part of leading a good life.

A Hindu funeral. The body is wrapped in a white sheet and then burnt, or cremated.

Festivals

Festivals are times when people meet together to celebrate something special. Your birthday is a festival. It celebrates the day you were born. All religions have festivals when people share and enjoy a special celebration.

Chinese New Year is celebrated with colourful processions in the street, music, dancing and monster dragons. Like many festivals, its religious meaning has been forgotten.

Some festivals celebrate important times of the year. For example, Hindus have a spring festival called Holi, when part of the fun is to spray people with coloured water. At harvest time, when all the crops have been gathered, people have festivals to thank God.

Some festivals are held in memory of holy people. Sikhs, Buddhists and Muslims all celebrate the birthdays of their founders. Christians do, too. They celebrate the birthday of Jesus at Christmas. Many religions have a festival of light, which people celebrate by lighting hundreds of candles.

Before a festival, there is sometimes a period when people do not eat. This is called a fast, and the fast ends with a special meal. At many festivals, people give presents to each other, and exchange greetings like 'Happy Divali' or 'Merry Christmas'. By joining in a festival, people share their faith and happy times.

Divali is a Hindu festival of lights. Candles and coloured lights are lit to celebrate the New Year.

GLOSSARY, BOOKS TO READ

A glossary is a word list. This one explains unusual words that are used in this book.

Celebration A way of showing that an event is special by doing something you enjoy.

Ceremony A set of actions done at some special event, like a marriage.

Church A Christian place of worship.

Cremate To burn a body after death, instead of burying it.

Custom The way certain things are usually done.

Faith Very strong belief.

Fast A time when people do not eat at all, or do not eat certain kinds of food, because it is part of their religion.

Gurdwara Temple where Sikhs meet for worship.

Holy A word to describe someone or something that is especially important in a religion.

Meditating A kind of deep thinking about something religious.

Mosque A Muslim place of worship.

Pilgrim A person who makes a journey to a sacred place.

Prayer Special thoughts or words that a person sends or says to God or to a god. Prayer can also be a way of listening to God.

Prophet A person who tells people about God and what God wants them to do.

Ritual A special set of actions done at certain times, that have a religious meaning.

Sacred A word to describe something that is very special and important in a religion; holy.

Scriptures The sacred writings of any religion.

Shrine Sacred place set aside for worship.

Symbol A sign, picture, object or action which stands for some special thing or idea.

Synagogue A Jewish place of worship.

Temple A holy place where people meet for worship.

Tradition Beliefs, customs and ideas that have continued for many years.

Worship A way of showing that someone or something has great worth and importance.

BOOKS TO READ

You can read more about religions in these books. Some of them are harder to read than this one, but they all have plenty of pictures.

Religions of the World series: **The Muslim World; The Hindu World; The Jewish World; The Christian World; The Buddhist World; The Sikh World; The New Religious World** all published by Macdonald Educational, 1982–5.

My Belief series: **I am a Jew; I am a Sikh; I am a Muslim; I am a Buddhist** and others, all published by Franklin Watts, 1984–5.

Exploring Religion: People; Buildings; Worship; Writings; Festivals; Signs and Symbols all by Olivia Bennett, Bell and Hyman, 1984.

Festivals by Beverley Birch, Macdonald Educational, 1984